just saying

Wesleyan Poetry

RAE ARMANTROUT

just saying

Wesleyan University Press

Middletown, Connecticut

Wesleyan University Press
Middletown CT 06459
www.wesleyan.edu/wespress
© 2013 Rae Armantrout
All rights reserved
Manufactured in the United States of America
Designed by Mindy Basinger Hill
Typeset in Calluna

Wesleyan University Press is a member of the Green
Press Initiative. The paper used in this book meets their
minimum requirement for recycled paper.

Library of Congress Cataloging-in-Publication Data

Armantrout, Rae, 1947–
Just saying / Rae Armantrout.—1st ed.
         p.   cm.—(Wesleyan Poetry Series)
Poems.
ISBN 978-0-8195-7299-8 (cloth: alk. paper)—
ISBN 978-0-8195-7300-1 (ebook)
I. Title.
PS3551.R455J87 2013
811'.54—dc23   2012024671

5   4   3   2   1

CONTENTS

ACKNOWLEDGMENTS

The author thanks the editors of the publications where these poems first appeared.

Custom. Chapbook. Ottawa: Above/Ground Press, 2012 (ed. Rob Mcclennan).

Anthologies

The Best American Poetry of 2012. New York: Scribner, 2012 (ed. Mark Doty and David Lehman). *The Open Door: One Hundred Poems, One Hundred Years of* Poetry *Magazine*. Chicago: University of Chicago Press, 2012 (ed. Don Share and Christian Wiman). *The New American Poetry of Engagement: A 21st Century Anthology*. Jefferson, N.C.: McFarland, 2012 (ed. Ann Keniston and Jeffrey Gray).

Magazines

Academy of American Poets Poem-a-Day Project, The Believer, Boston Review Online, Chicago Review, Colorado Review, Conjunctions, Denver Quarterly, Dublin Poetry Review, Eleven Eleven, Esque, Fence, Jacket2, Lana Turner, The Nation, The New Yorker, 1913, Plame, Poetry, Quarterly West, Rampike, Salzburg Review, Shampoo, Smartish Pace, Swan's Rag, Westwind Review

just saying

SCRIPTURE

Your violins pursue
the downhill course
of streams,

even to their wild
curls and cowlicks.

To repeat
is not to catch.

✹

Consider the hummingbirds,
how they're gussied up

and monomaniacal
as the worst (or best)
of you.

Consider the bright,
streamlined emergency
they manifest.

✹

My leaves form bells,
topknots,
small cups of sex,

overweening, unstoppered.

Not one of you
with all your practice

is so extravagantly
coiffed.

INSTEAD

1

To each his own
severance package.

The Inca
hacked large stones
into the shapes of
nearby peaks.

2

The eerie thing
is that ghosts don't exist.

Rows
of clear droplets
hang from stripped twigs

instead.

3

Pain brings attention
to herself.

Spine on Fire!
Trail Blazer!

(Thinks she's hot.)

Out here
slim trunks bend
every which

OLD SCHOOL

Pull strings taut and
something like
points reappear
in the model.

Take place. Momentum
is conserved. Carry
elementary clone world
punctuation. Hostile

fetus. Cancer
is old school.
Impersonal. Carry
imperial aspirations.

To aspirate
is to breathe in
and choke. Nobody
wants this.

"Nobody did this
to me," screams
now blind Cyclops.
Nobody's listening

is conserved.

DRESS UP

To be "dressed"
is to emit
"virtual particles."

*

The spirit of "renormalization" is that

an electron
all by itself

can have infinite
mass and charge,

but, when it's "dressed" . . .

*

A toddler stares at us
till we look up.

"Flirtatious," we call it.

She waits
until we get the joke

about being here,
being there.

ACCOUNTS

for Brian Keating

Light was on its way
from nothing
to nowhere.

Light was all business

    Light was full speed

when it got interrupted.

Interrupted by what?

When it got tangled up
and broke
into opposite

    broke into brand-new things.

    What kinds of things?

    Drinking Cup

      "Thinking of you!
              Convenience Valet"

How could speed take shape?

*

Hush!
Do you want me to start over?

*

The fading laser pulse

Information describing the fading laser pulse

is stored

is encoded

in the spin states
of atoms.

God
is balancing his checkbook

God is encrypting his account.

This is taking forever!

EVENT HORIZON

A street person? –
unshaven, haggard –
in a button-down
and a full black skirt.

If an image could talk,
what would it say?

A man in a skirt participates.

A man in a skirt
is never alone?

✳

We are never alone.

We are men in skirts.

I am.

I draw attention
to myself.

To make a black hole,
one must concentrate.

COLD

What does it take
to stay warm?

Fire in a cage,
gnawing on wood,

throwing sprite
after sprite

off
to extinction.

Each baby's soul
is cute
in the same way.

Rapt attention
on a stalk,

surprised by thirst.

JUST SAYING

What might be said

to disport itself

along the cinderblock

in leaves.

     ✳

What I write

I write instead

of ivy,

     ✳

Green snouts

in evidence or –

more

to the point –

insolent

and tense.

*

What might be said

to writhe

professionally

as the days

nod and wink.

GHOSTED

1

Long, loose,
spindly, green
stalks with their few
leaves, bug-eaten
tatters
on which
a black monarch
sits, folding
and unfolding
its wings.

2

A friend's funeral has broken up –

or was that the last dream?

Now I'm struggling
between monuments,

looking for Chuck.

It's getting dark
and I'm pissed off

because he won't answer his cell.

3

On the wall in a coffee bar,
a model's arms
and stern, pretty face
frame a window

(where her chest should be)

and a clear sky beyond

REMAINDER

String of empty offices,
illuminated, festive?

*

People exist
to attach importance.

*

I practice
high speed de-
selection.

*

The difference

between nothing
and nothingness

is existence.

＊

My dead friends
don't visit me;

they say I didn't
know them.

＊

You are cautious
indolent, stubborn,
skeptical, gentle, tense.

＊

At sunset, pigeons
practice synchronized flying.

＊

Thus "are" becomes "is,"
"is" becomes "ness."

＊

Let the burning spill
extend

SUGGESTION

Your brain feels swollen,
as if it's floating
on a string, no, on two,
each held in the balled fist
of an eye.

The feeling produces this image:
two crying children –
brother and sister? –
clutching strings
in an old city of brick, stone.

What does this image explain?

*

"In the beginning"
In the end,
these are –
        there are –
only suggestions:

"Clockwise" or "counter" –
though there are no clocks.
"Horizontal" or "vertical" –
though there is no horizon.

*

Being aware of anything outside yourself
means you aren't sleeping

so you have pushed things away.
Now you are alone with pain.

Pain is as large as you are
and is not obedient.

If you *became* pain, perhaps,
then you could rest.

But it is not possible
to merge with pain.

SPENT

Suffer as in allow.

List as in want.

Listless as in transcending
desire, or not rising
to greet it.

To list
is to lean,
dangerously,
to one side.

Have you forgotten?

Spent
as in exhausted.

MY TASTE

What it means
to "own sake."

✳

How to explain
my taste
for phone lines,

the shared slouch
of those two

or this one
like a ruler

where a hummingbird
marks the center
            slash.

✳

This yard which
for years
was a blond patch

and is now
a stylish desert,
bronze crushed granite

between bushes
flowering furiously

HAUNTS

I

Rock eaten
to familiar shapes –

heads cocked
on jagged spines.

✳

How many
orange, pink, white
rock pinnacles
are visible from here?

Grandeur
is that number

plus distance,

as if "again"
could be made manifest.

2

"Nature" was a 19th-century fad,
 cousin to eugenics.

In the 21st century,
America's soft core's
undead.

*

On how many bookstore shelves,
lovely, fanged teenagers,
red-eyed, smeared with blood.

PARTING SHOTS

I

Long, confident sentences
of the early visitors,

so unlike ours,
so much like one another,

remark
on the sculpted "grandeur"

of the walls,
and then, with one light touch,

on the bracing sense
of insignificance

that they impart.

2

Behind the only wall in sight,
the defamiliarized wall,

a sniper
tells a camera crew

his work is "invigorating"
because it's "personal."

INFLECTION

When I wake up, I'm dragging
lower incisors
along those above,

and, for an instant,
I experience
satisfaction and fear

in equal parts.

✳

I'm reading, "The wrath of God
inflicts dragons,
ostriches,
and owls,
seductively singing."

Go on.

✳

Babble:

horns punctuate
a flexible roar.

*

Some roofs have one
or more

water tanks
with pointed hats;

some roofs have none.

Some squares are black
and trimmed in silver;

some are gray.

THE LOOK

The boxer crab
attaches a sea anemone
to each claw,
waves.

＊

You, small flower-bearing stick,
what is your true name?

＊

Spooked and spooked again.
It's cute

when the intricately patterned
black and yellow fish

twitches
and shoots off

in a new direction.

＊

From birth,
you've been moving

your eyes
back and forth,

looking
to be hailed.

AT LEAST

I

Water-strider, pond skater,
Jesus bug

skitters across the surface
tension

and

the "least-area surface"
(flat, smooth)

has a surface tension
of zero.

2

This train of thought
is not a train,

but a tendril,
                blind.

It's a line
of ants
following a scent trail.

Or a string of stragglers
on a death march.

3

"Go cloud!"
 says the stranded

traveler (actress)

with that small fist pump

now used
to indicate
irony's uselessness.

HOLDING PEN

Wall-mounted sconces
hold thought bubbles up

on either side of a
bed, mirror, television.

*

You laugh
when the man
mentions something
you recognize.

*

Wavy brown lines
forming squares
on a carpet;

some squashed,
some bloated!

*

Hold that thought

for what remains
of time

SUBDIVISION

In a horror movie
the dead eat the living;

while in reality
the living eat the dead.

*

To matter (verb)
is to be
of concern;

matter is that
which possesses
"rest mass."

*

You've been living
in a false
vacuum,

one composed of
"of,"

extensively subdivided.

Balanced

MY APOCALYPSE

A woman writes to ask
how far along I am
with my apocalypse.

What will you give me
if I tell?

An origami fish
made from a dollar bill.

After the apocalypse,
we will all be in a band.

We will understand each other
perfectly.

✳

"It's alright" and

"It doesn't matter."

Let "it" stand
for nothing.

✳

A weathered, fleshy bicyclist
wearing bunny ears
and a tie-dyed shirt
says "Zoom"
as she coasts past

THINGS

1

He grabbed the doctor's finger
with his eyes
and he was going for a ride,
whipped back and forth,
for the first time
like a   like a
Or was this digit
one of the things –
but what are those –
he had been sent
to find?

2

It is one thing
to say that experience
is discontinuous
and another
to say that it is
imaginary
at both ends.

3

As if the light
at the end of
tunnel vision
were the glare
of the delivery room
pulled
from memory's
grab bag;

as if we'd come
full circle,
so to speak, though
this time
no one was talking

ENTRY

"You'll

have to come through

me":

block letters
on a placard
waved at an eager
camera crew –

and then we're clear.

     ✳

Children prefer counterfactuals.

     ✳

Plump legs pump
orange pedals
at top speed,

turning the corner,

powered by what
elective identity?

✶

In a dream, you can't say,
"Ezra Pound

appears to be
in love

with what looks like
a beautiful Black call-girl."

In dreams,
things are understood

(to be) as
they appear.

ARRIVALS

Sign in the airport:
It's not how much
Cloud,
but what kind.

*

Welcome.

"We don't play requests,
but we don't play bagpipes
either. We figure
that's fair."

That's the bad-boy
sass
of globalization

kick-starting you
on Clear Channel

where even the spin
gets spun.

*

Here's one:

The devil is a blowsy,
failed executive

who fires burn-outs,
star after star.

*

Every known object
rotates

as if:

       b. keeping busy
       c. stunned

CIRCULATING

See something, say something.

Jotting in a notebook.

Carrying oneself
in a defensive posture.

Pausing before shop windows.

Half-hearted
self-surveillance.

Say something.

"Purpose-driven."

"Normal circulation pattern."

Rate monitor.

Jotting in a notebook.

PRODUCTION

Crowd of wracked
spindles

cannot cover
desert "floor."

That throng of extras?

Hired mourners in costume.

✳

B-list snits
as white noise.

Old grievances are re-enacted
and aired

while "fracking"
blasts gas from shale.

✳

Kid
scared of her own

shadow – natch –

that access-denied
body.

BEING SEEN

Old-time
Loony Tunes
heart-shaped
tin

on which
Tweety Bird,
beak agape,
eyes bulging,

holds a
Valentine's Day
card against
his own thin

breast.

*

Here's the best part:

sky at the horizon
blood red. Not really.

Darker and topped
with a swathe

of peach
above which

a black cloud
like a submarine

and like big beads
on a string

is now nowhere
to be seen

TRANSACTIONS

1

What do we like best
about ourselves?

Our inability
to be content.

We might see this
restlessness

as a chip
not yet cashed in.

2

You appear
because you're lonely

maybe.
You would not say that.

You come to tell me
you're saving money
by cooking for yourself.

You've figured out
what units you'll need

to exchange for units
if you intend

I know I mustn't
interrupt.

    3

Hectic and flexible,

flames

are ideal

new bodies for us!

AT

1

"*I* define terror,"
the shooter says

and types out the dictionary.

The government controls us
through grammar
and new currency.

2

Red car

at the center
of the circle maze

formed by an illegible
white sentence.

On the black wall
of the Hyundai building

block letters shout:
SNAP OUT OF IT

but I can't see
what they're driving at

ACTION POEM

1

On screen
men discover
that their mothers
are imposters,
that their world's
unreal.

Substitution
is eerie.

(We discover *this* again.)

2

America
has a lucid dream.

She's falling
from level
to collapsing level
in someone else's (whose?)
terrain, through
floorboards, off bridges,
firing desperately.

Someone says, "Dream
bigger," handing us
an RPG.

THE THINNING

1

These guys try to make us
match moods to products

the way once,
under love's spell,

we attached meaning
to sound,

attached sounds to objects.

The old magic won't work now,

but it's nice
to be reminded of it.

2

She's a tease,
tears her skirts off

one by one.
Really?

Drops her petals
as if she could always
make more.

It's tiresome.

We know
what she looks like
naked.

On a cold night,
we can see forever.

ELEMENTS OF BLANK

You're not selling the product,
you're selling commitment.

*

Somehow we know that the cover girl has just lifted her
head, looked into the lens by accident. Her light eyes
are those of a lion raising its head from a carcass. (Her
tousled blond hair reinforces this effect.) A moment ago,
it seems, she was absorbed in something all-consuming,
draining. Clearly, her gaze only appears to take us in.

*

Get them to opt out
of what's available
apart from the experience
of our product.

*

To take a flight is to make a decision which can't be rescinded.
That in itself is enough to inspire fear. But it isn't wise to show
weakness. Now our fate is bound by momentum to that of the
people around us, people we did not choose, would not have
chosen. We await the beverage tray. When it comes, we will
once again have a number of options.

SITUATION

I

A passenger and a waiter
walk into a situation.

A passenger waits.

A traveler, accompanied by children, remarks
that the waiter is "pretty demanding.
You'll see."

"This is pretty crazy, huh?
See what I'm doing
all day long?"

(What?)

"This."

2

On each tile
four pink ovals

(petals)

point to the cardinal
directions

3

The pendulum has swung
toward finding absorption sites
for secondary toxins.

Films which depict
humans gaining enhanced powers
through exposure to chemical spills
or to radiation.

Repetitive motor movement;
avoiding eye contact

MIDST

We're all saying the same thing now,

scolding the same shadow,

not in harmony,
but in sync

or by turns.

Singing that bar
about the flock
taking off

"as if"
it were one body –

as if this was one body –

and who could be listening?

REPRESENTATIVE

I

It begins as a polyp.

In the shape of a headless man,
it marches along the sea floor.

Where this man steps,
another man will grow.

When the water's warm,
his wrists break off,

clear round by round, and,
dangling tentacles,

push upward
(outward, inward),

easy as breathing
until you think

2

We're reading words
we don't remember writing,

words that aren't words at all,

bluffing it through
to scattered applause

down the long
seminar table.

3

White veined
with wandering blue;

blue seamed
with white.

That heaven could be built
out of the names of gems!

"Agate" and "Amethyst."

What did they represent?

SECOND ORDER

Certainly
I distinguish myself
from what I hear

and from what I overhear
myself think.

Rarefied elements
enjoy auspices.

Be specific.

The sun
swallows itself
or what is nearest?

Shines.

SCALE

1

In my youth, I craved the small picture,

the autistic strung-out
hearts of ivy, star jasmine,

the "on and on"
without budging.

I liked Russian icons,

circles
within circles in

the virgin's halo,
the way her cloak

matched the sky which
was not the sky at all.

2

Now I see
that the outsized "personalities"

of our day,
the Brad and Angies,

have the blurred, grainy texture
indicative of stretching.

We get a faint ping
back
when we focus on these objects.

     3

"An electron
is an excitation

in an electron field,"

a permanent tizzy
in the presence of

what?

Like thought
it creates the ground
it covers,

like thought,
it can't stop

CUSTOM

We maintain a critical distance
from the sad spaniel gentlemen

in cravats
on the plaid duvet

at the Custom Hotel,
Los Angeles.

We are so over it.
We fly

from terminal
to terminal

almost endlessly.

We are almost
money.

We can wait
at high speed.

AND

1

Tense and *tenuous*
grow from the same root

as does *tender*
in its several guises:

the sour grass flower;
the yellow moth.

2

I would not confuse
the bogus
with the spurious.

The bogus
is a sore thumb,

while the spurious
pours forth

as fish and circuses.

TREATMENT

The relationship between a handsome young broker
and a lovely young curator
is in trouble.
Before they can marry, he must
come to tolerate,
then feel guarded affection for
a good-natured buffoon
who populates dioramas
with stuffed mouse couples in period dress,
then for an assortment of others,
some less likeable,
who also take passionate interest
in an activity that generates no profit.

COMING OUT

1

The Alphas, The Incredibles, The X-Men,
characters with freak abilities,
are being suppressed,
regulated,
in the name of society,
until, finally,
they break out, use
their power
as they please.

Now, for "ability"
read *wealth*.

2

Say you're hiding nothing.

Say blood creeps
through your skeleton,

which is upright,
gnarled, brown,

and hung with a thousand
clean slates

3

Let's not rationalize taste!

A mound
of dark

loose dirt
with a small hole

on top:
a *pucker*

WATCH THIS

1

Small flame wandering
on its wick.

2

I had wanted
intimacy, for you to see
what I saw
in my mirror.

3

Pleasure preferred
in semblance,

sibilance

EXPERTS

1

I met a genius.
He's an expert on tourniquets.

No, turncoats.

No, tunicates.

He knows everything
there is to know
about sea squirts.

He knows what it's like

2

We coordinate our thrusts
by habit
to minimize distraction.

If an algorithm
has proved useful,

we believe in one
god.

We close our eyes
or stare

at a nonexistent
horizon

as if listening
for something vital,

faint,

some emerging
consensus
in the background chatter.

When certainty is high,
we grunt or yelp –

the agreed-upon signal.

One of us does.

EXPERIMENTAL DESIGN

To test for consciousness,
ask the machine,

"What is wrong
with this picture?"

A potted plant
where a keyboard should be.

Ask yourself,
"Would a cat be frightened?"

MEETING EXPECTATIONS

Full frontal purple
discs, small flowers
of the potato vine,

so wide open
they're flat.

*

A pigeon's ritual pecks
at the concrete.

Satisfactory.

So you say,
"Facts are facts."

*

In order to produce this
piercing, hysterical laugh,

a woman shocks her infant
again and again

with a green parrot
hand puppet.

PROBLEM AREAS

Descended
from the peacock's
blind eyes

and the chimp's
acute suspicions,

we invented astrology

to give purpose
to the stars.

✳

We've been raptured

to our fathers' shoulders
where we've hidden

the past in the future,
the future in the past.

✳

Now time is continuous.

We must renounce
each breath.

BETWEEN ISLANDS

1

If every eighth element
listed by atomic weight

is noxious,

is that proof of
intelligent design?

2

Here's your far-fetched plan,
glinting
in slanted light –

except "plan" is wrong.

Thought comes before
or after,

but you interpose
yourself

and that red hourglass
which you think nothing of.

3

Next to the thoroughfare,

between the shopping plaza
and the medical complex,

a man in a straw hat
leans
on a pink
pasteboard sign

with one
woman's shoe on it

and the word "Repair"

HALF LIVES

In coordinated universal time,

a second

is a decimal

place between two

ground states

of the cesium . . .

Seizure?

Do you know

how you got here?

Little center-stitched scrap

of white. Madcap,

veering off.

Is there something better?

PROGRESS

The thickness of sleep,

the sense of swarm,
of nebulous propagation

from which we wake
by narrowing,

"sharpening,"

our focus.

        *

The three weird sisters
are you,

babbling, in drag,

and what's so strange
about that?

They foresee your downfall,
but urge you on.

Where is there to go
but down?

You want to go,
don't you?

*

If we think dying
is like falling

asleep,
then we believe

wrongly, rightly
that it's a way

of sinking into
what happens,

joining the program
in progress

THE MUSIC TEACHER

In a room full of empty music stands, drum kits,
a plump young man in a cardigan
strums a guitar and sings about
(lists) the articles of clothing
your kids will need to get
at Target.

The list is redundant, generic.
His singing is slightly off-key.

Buying these clothes is one of the many
tasks you'll perform,

be a good sport about.

You and your children are in it together.

WITHOUT END

"There is no obstacle

to appropriate types

of information processors

continuing to process

information."

✳

"Process" meaning register;

register meaning process.

✳

"Or more simply

they could process

infinite amounts

of information

in an unbounded future."

*

Process meaning separate;

process meaning fuse.

*

Coral

feather-duster

flowers

of the eucalyptus

hang among

gray-greens.

*

"Which is not to say

that they would

or should."

BARDOS

I

Some say the soul
hangs from the ceiling
when the doctor pronounces
the body dead

and, afterwards, perhaps,
watches crises
in the lives of strangers,
bored

as we are here.

2

Let volume speak volumes.

One claims
he can recreate the sound
of a family argument
using bankrupt fishermen
and oil execs
to represent dead relatives.

3

One uses leathery
maroon tongues,
writhing,
laced up both sides
with gray shark-tooth spines.

4

I've been telling someone
(a cipher
emphatically)

how unfair it is
that so-and-so, a killer,
is angry

at his boyfriend/girlfriend
(unclear)

for being a "truck-stop whore"
when

LIVING SPACE

Struck bell's
old well;

long vowel's
vanishing circumference.

✳

Hawking says gravity
pulled all this
from nothing.

✳

Maroon curtains
swept into flounces,
held by brass barrettes

beyond which
a cinderblock wall
wears an ivy wig.

*

But gravity
is the impression

matter makes
on space.

*

Or gravity
is self-love

LUSTER

What flickers
with some delicacy

of feeling,

some hesitancy –
and then persists.

＊

What circles. What darts.

＊

Hunger

is like the inside
biting you.

"Like" is like
insomnia.

＊

These green cherry tomatoes;
their false pregnancies,

staked. Lustrous.

＊

"That's all I meant."

All I meant by
"witches."

FORMAL CONSTRAINTS

Now the poem

is saying

what it is forced to say

by its history, its form

thus pleasing the reader,

who knows he can trust it

without being obliged

to regard

any statements it may make

as accurate

or "true."

The poem is ridding itself

and us

of the burden

of abstraction –

a valuable service.

Still

a question arises

as to how

to dispose of the poem

once this divestment

is complete.

ROUNDS

We are exchanging
futures.

Hand me the remote.

✳

Silver points
the Xmas tree is making.

Small white lights
smeared into points.

✳

Sky says, "La, la, la."

"Hark!" and

"Told you so!"

MOTHER'S DAY

I wring the last
sweetness

from syllables
and consume it before you.

*

I make sense
like a scorpion

and the sun
will be smitten.

*

If I appear to address you
while quoting an old text,

I am indistinguishable
from nature

and therefore sublime.

*

If I reveal myself
mercilessly,

what will I not transcend?

*

Like God, I will leave

an arc
of implication

THUS

1

What's sufficient?

Coy threats
addressed to a captive?

Unaccountable florescence.

Silent pink trumpets.

Mention.

Mention me again.

2

Thought you followed
someone else's thought,
thought you saw
where it was going
or, if not, could
hold the expected
turn
and the actual trajectory
side by side
for an instant

thus:

a shadow,
"Pleasantly surprised."

FOCUS

The point at which
an object
must be situated

in order
to be well defined.

✳

The situation in which
a point

can be defined
as an object.

✳

Clipped nonce?

Far-flung.

✳

Hibiscus
can think

purple whorls
around us

THE ELECT

I want to explore
the post-hope zeitgeist.

I don't like
the option
of zero wiggle room.

I might mean
"I'm next,"

or "in the vicinity
                    of,"
or "about to"

move my joystick sideways,

register
for the long

interglacial
moraine.

NEW INTELLIGENCE

1

Stars
are the campfires
of exiles.

Language exists
to pull things
close.

✳

Stop that!

Communications
are being monitored.

Collusion is forbidden.

Humanity
will be punished

with the profusion
of new jargons.

2

Inverted in glass,
a white cup
invents the underworld.

*

Fog thins
to chiffon,

nylon,

Easter.

*

In the universe next door,
I'm gone

and the shadows
of the leaves

of the elm I had pulled down

still make a fuss
over the earth.

ANOTHER

Brittle ovals,

pinkish gray
and thin,

hang
in shoals,

treading currents.

✳

Eucalyptus,
let us in.

STILL AND ALL

1

Since we've grown,
it's reasonable to think
we're shape-shifters,

that the pink hibiscus
with its protruding stamen
is a French kiss

we might still exchange.

✱

Sun laminates
the shallows

and an old woman
is dressed in gold lamé.

2

The sea's white blurts
do all the talking

here,
lift the weight

I only then
begin to feel.

*

Still,
in my nightmare

the doors all
look alike.

REAL TIME

Now the screen shows the tops of clouds
roiling
in time-lapse photography.

     ✳

She is in the Woodlawn Room.
It's a green cube

where a large ceramic frog
in jodhpurs

holds a lamp shade up
with its muscular arms.

When time stands still,
she hates herself.

Even a black hole
boils off.

Outside, a voice says,
"Ed,
are you ready to go home?"

She thinks it's ironic
when remarks

are not addressed to her.

✳

The cube hums
to itself.

MEANT

When the rat rests,
its brain

runs the maze again,
then runs it backwards,

and repeats.

This is early
music.

✳

"Poetry wants
to make things mean

more than they mean,"
says someone,

as if we knew
how much things meant

and in what unit
of measure.

＊

Some chords (crowds)
seem sad –

because uncertain? –

while others
appear quite resolved

HYMN

To put one over
                    on
        one.

     ✶

One is everywhere
lured

into branching again
in miniature:

espaliered chorus.

     ✶

"Glory be to him,"
sing voices
that can't quite dissolve

in tears,
as mist.

     ✶

Incremental hum.

Collapse on cue.

Praise Sisyphus.

STOP AND GO

1

Long burst of tweets.

We wait to see
if it picks up again

from the same place –

the place we came from?

2

Stop,
I know this one.

It goes
everything's

a metaphor
for sensation.

ABOUT THE AUTHOR

Rae Armantrout is a professor of writing and literature at the University of California, San Diego, and the author of eleven books of poetry, most recently *Money Shot* (2011) and *Versed* (2009). The latter was awarded the 2010 Pulitzer Prize for Poetry.